MAX LUCADO

GOD'S MIRROR

A MODERN PARABLE

Reflecting the
Father's Heart

MAX LUCADO

GOD'S MIRROR

A MODERN PARABLE

INTEGRITY
PUBLISHERS

Reflecting the
Father's Heart

GOD'S MIRROR

PART ONE

REFLECTING HIS HEART

"*So you like* Jewish authors?"

1

REFLECTING HIS HEART

"So you like Jewish authors?"

The fellow asking the question sat on the aisle seat.
I had the window, which meant I had a view of the
runway. The mechanical crew was repairing a bird
dent on the wing. While they worked, I read. As I read
my Bible, the rabbi interrupted.

"So, you like Jewish authors?"

The twinkle in his eye betrayed his pleasure in the question. His chest-length mop of a beard couldn't hide his smile. I had spotted him earlier in the waiting area. The tassels from his shirttail and hair-clipped yarmulke led me to peg him as the pious, silent type.

Pious. Yes. But silent? He loved to talk. He loved to talk Torah. I was in for a lesson.

TUCKED AWAY *in the* CEREMONIES
and LAWS *of* MOSES *are*
PICTURES *of* GOD.

Tucked away in the ceremonies and laws of Moses, he explained, are pictures of God. Who could offer a sacrifice and not weep for God's grace? Who could read about servants redeeming their kinsmen and not think about God redeeming us? And who could read the third commandment without remembering to live for God's glory?

I signaled a time-out, opened to Exodus, and read the third command:

"*You* SHALL NOT TAKE *the* NAME

of *the* **LORD** YOUR GOD

in VAIN ... " EXODUS 20:7 (NKJV)

My puzzled expression was enough to request an

explanation.

"Don't think language; think lifestyle," he instructed.
"The command calls us to elevate the name or

reputation of God to the highest place. We exist to

give honor to his name. May I illustrate?"

By now the damaged wing was fixed (the plane's;

can't speak for the bird). And as we gained altitude,

so did the rabbi. I took notes. He proceeded to

WE EXIST *to* GIVE HONOR
to HIS NAME.

create a story involving a Manhattan skyscraper.

Everyone in the building works for the CEO, whose

office is on the top floor. Most have not seen him,

but they have seen his daughter. She works in the

building for her father. She exploits her family

position to her benefit.

One morning she approaches Bert, the guard.

"I'm hungry, Bert. Go down the street and buy

me a danish."

The demand places Bert in a quandary. He's on duty.

Leaving his post puts the building at risk. But his

boss's daughter insists, "Come on, now; hurry up."

What option does he have? As he leaves, he says

nothing but thinks something like,

<hr />

IF *the* DAUGHTER *is* SO BOSSY,

WHAT DOES *that* SAY ABOUT HER FATHER?

She's only getting started. Munching on her muffin, she bumps into a paper-laden secretary. "Where are you going with all those papers?"

"To have them bound for an afternoon meeting."

"Forget the meeting. Come to my office and vacuum the carpet."

"But I was told … "

"And I am telling you something else."

The woman has no choice. After all, this is the boss's daughter speaking, which causes the secretary to question the wisdom of the boss.

And on the daughter goes. Making demands. Calling shots. Interrupting schedules. Never invoking the name of her dad. Never leveraging her comments with, "My dad said … "

No need to.

Isn't she the boss's child? Doesn't the child speak for the father? And so Bert abandons his post. An assistant fails to finish a task. And more than one employee questions the wisdom of the man upstairs. *Does he really know what he is doing?* they wonder.

The rabbi paused here. We both felt the plane nosing downward. His remaining time was short. But his point was clear. The girl dishonored the name of her father, not with vulgar language, but with insensitive living.

KEEP THIS UP *and the* WHOLE

BUILDING *will be*

SECOND-GUESSING *the* CEO.

But my traveling partner wasn't finished, as

he proposed, "But what if the daughter acted

differently?" and then proceeded to recast the story.

Rather than demand a muffin from Bert, she brings

a muffin to Bert. "I thought of you this morning,"

she explains. "You arrive so early. Do you have time

to eat?" And she hands him the gift.

En route to the elevator she bumps into a woman

with an armful of documents. "My, I'm sorry. Can I

help?" the daughter offers. The assistant smiles, and the two carry the stacks down the hallway.

And so the daughter engages the people. She asks about their families. Offers to bring them coffee. New workers are welcomed, and hard workers are applauded. She, through kindness and concern, raises the happiness level of the entire company.

She does so not even mentioning her father's name. Never does she declare, "My father says … " There is no need to. Is she not his child? Does she not speak

on his behalf? Reflect his heart? When she speaks,

they assume she speaks for him. And because they

think highly of her, they think highly of her father.

They've not seen him.

They've not met him.

But they know his child, so they know his heart.

THEY'VE NOT *seen* HIM.
THEY'VE NOT *met* HIM.
BUT THEY *know* HIS CHILD,
SO THEY *know* HIS HEART.

By now the flight was ending and so was my Hebrew lesson. Thanks to the rabbi, the third command shouldered new meaning. Paul, another rabbi, would have appreciated the point. He wrote:

"WE *are* AMBASSADORS *for* CHRIST, *as* THOUGH GOD *were* MAKING *an* APPEAL THROUGH US ... " 2 CORINTHIANS 5:20 (NASB)

The AMBASSADOR *has a*

SINGULAR AIM —

to REPRESENT *his* KING.

He promotes the king's agenda, protects the king's reputation, and presents the king's will. The ambassador elevates the name of the king.

I pray that we do the same. May God rescue us from self-centered thinking. May we have no higher goal than to see someone think more highly of our Father, our King.

"You know how the story ends?" the rabbi asked as we were taxiing to a stop. Apparently he had a punch line.

"No, I don't. How?"

"The daughter takes the elevator to the top floor to see her father. When she arrives, he is waiting in the doorway. He's aware of her good works and has seen her kind acts. People think more highly of him because of her. And he knows it. As she approaches, he greets her with six words."

The rabbi paused and smiled.

"What are they?" I urged, never expecting to hear an

orthodox Jew quote Jesus.

"Well done, good and faithful servant."

MAY *you* REFLECT *the* FATHER'S HEART

UNTIL *you* HEAR *the* SAME.

"WELL DONE, GOOD *and*

FAITHFUL SERVANT." Matthew 25:23 (niv)

PART TWO

REFLECTING HIS GLORY

This COULD *be* HIS ONLY

CHANCE *for* ESCAPE.

G. R. Tweed looked across the Pacific waters at the American ship on the horizon. Brushing the jungle sweat from his eyes, the young naval officer swallowed deeply and made his decision. This could be his only chance for escape.

Tweed had been hiding on Guam for nearly three years. When the Japanese occupied the island in 1941, he ducked into the thick tropical brush. Survival hadn't been easy, but he preferred the swamp to a POW camp.

Late in the day July 10, 1944, he spotted the friendly vessel. He scurried up a hill and positioned himself on a cliff. Reaching into his pack, he pulled out a small mirror. At 6:20 p.m., he began sending signals. Holding the edge of the mirror in his fingers, he tilted it back and forth, bouncing the sunrays in the direction of the boat. Three short flashes. Three long. Three short again. Dot-dot-dot. Dash-dash-dash. Dot-dot-dot. SOS.

Three SHORT FLASHES.

Three LONG. *Three* SHORT AGAIN.

SOS

The signal caught the eyes of a sailor on board the USS *McCall*. A rescue party boarded a motorized dinghy and slipped into the cove past the coastal guns. Tweed was rescued.

He was glad to have that mirror, glad he knew how to use it, and glad that the mirror cooperated. Suppose it hadn't. (Prepare yourself for a crazy thought.) Suppose the mirror had resisted, pushed its own agenda. Rather than reflect a message from the sun, suppose it had opted to send its own.

SUPPOSE *the* MIRROR

had RESISTED, *pushed* ITS

OWN AGENDA.

After all, three years of isolation would leave one starved for attention. Rather than sending an SOS, the mirror could have sent an LAM. "Look at me."

An egotistical mirror?

The only crazier thought would be an insecure mirror. *What if I blow it? What if I send a dash when I'm supposed to send a dot? Besides, have you seen the blemishes on my surface?* Self-doubt could paralyze a mirror.

SELF-DOUBT *could*

PARALYZE *a* MIRROR.

So could self-pity. *Been crammed down in that pack, lugged through jungles, and now, all of a sudden expected to face the bright sun and perform a crucial service? No way. Staying in the pack. Not getting any reflection out of me.*

Good thing Tweed's mirror didn't have a mind of its own.

But God's mirrors? Unfortunately, we do.

We are his mirrors, you know. Tools of heaven's

heliography. Reduce the human job description down to one phrase, and this is it: Reflect God's glory. As Paul wrote:

"*And* WE, *with* OUR UNVEILED FACES REFLECTING LIKE MIRRORS *the* BRIGHTNESS *of the* LORD, ALL GROW BRIGHTER *and* BRIGHTER *as* WE *are* TURNED INTO *the* IMAGE THAT WE REFLECT; THIS *is the* WORK *of the* LORD WHO IS SPIRIT."

2 CORINTHIANS 3:18 (JB)

Reflect GOD'S GLORY.

Some reader just arched an eyebrow. *Wait a second, you are thinking. I've read that passage before, more than once. And it sounded different.* Indeed it may have. Perhaps it's because you are used to reading it in a different translation. "But we all, with unveiled face, *beholding as in a mirror* the glory of the Lord, are being transformed into the same image from glory to glory, just as from the Lord, the Spirit" (JB; emphasis mine).

One translation says, "beholding as in a mirror"; another says, "reflecting like mirrors." One implies contemplation; the other implies refraction. Which is accurate?

Actually both. The verb *katoptrizo* can be translated either way. Translators are in both camps:

"with unveiled face, *beholding*" (RSV)

"*beholding* as in a glass" (KJV)

"*reflecting* like mirrors" (JB)

"be mirrors that brightly *reflect*" (TLB)

"we ... all *reflect* the Lord's glory" (NIV)

But which meaning did Paul intend? In the context of the passage, Paul paralleled the Christian experience to the Mount Sinai experience of Moses. After the patriarch *beheld* the glory of God, his face *reflected* the glory of God. "The people of Israel could not bear to look at Moses' face. For his face shone with the glory of God" (2 Corinthians 3:7 NLT).

The face of Moses was so dazzling white that "the people of Israel could no more look right at him than stare into the sun" (2 Corinthians 3:7 MSG).

Upon beholding God, Moses could not help but reflect God. *The brightness he saw was the brightness he became.* Beholding led to becoming. Becoming led to reflecting. Perhaps the answer to the translation question, then, is "yes."

Did Paul mean "beholding as in a mirror"? Yes.

The BRIGHTNESS HE SAW

was the BRIGHTNESS HE BECAME.

Did Paul mean "reflecting like a mirror"? Yes.

Could it be that the Holy Spirit intentionally selected a verb that would remind us to do both? To behold God so intently we can't help but reflect him?

What does it mean to behold your face in a mirror? A quick glance? A casual look? No. To behold is to study, to stare, to contemplate. Beholding God's glory, then, is no side look or occasional glance; this beholding is a serious pondering.

GLIMPSES *of the* GLORY *of* GOD ...

Isn't that what we have done? We have camped at
the foot of Mount Sinai and beheld the glory of
God. Wisdom unsearchable. Purity unspotted. Years
unending. Strength undaunted. Love immeasurable.
Glimpses of the glory of God.

As we behold his glory, dare we pray that we, like
Moses, will reflect it? Dare we hope to be mirrors in
the hands of God, the reflection of the light of God?
This is the call.

"*Whatever* YOU DO, DO ALL
to the GLORY *of* GOD."

1 CORINTHIANS 10:31 (NKJV)

WHATEVER. WHATEVER.

LET YOUR MESSAGE

REFLECT GOD'S GLORY.

"LET *your* LIGHT SHINE *before* MEN,

that THEY *may* SEE YOUR GOOD DEEDS *and*

PRAISE YOUR FATHER *in* HEAVEN."

MATTHEW 5:16 (NIV)

LET YOUR SALVATION REFLECT GOD'S GLORY.

"HAVING BELIEVED, YOU WERE

MARKED *in* HIM WITH *a* SEAL,

the PROMISED HOLY SPIRIT, WHO IS *a*

DEPOSIT GUARANTEEING *our* INHERITANCE

UNTIL *the* REDEMPTION *of* THOSE WHO

are GOD'S POSSESSION—TO *the* PRAISE

of HIS GLORY."

EPHESIANS 1:13-14 (NIV)

LET YOUR BODY REFLECT GOD'S GLORY.

"YOU *are* NOT YOUR OWN ...

GLORIFY GOD *in* YOUR BODY ... "

1 CORINTHIANS 6:19-20 (NASB)

YOUR STRUGGLES HONOR GOD.

"THESE SUFFERINGS *of* OURS ARE FOR YOUR BENEFIT. AND *the* MORE *of* YOU WHO ARE WON *to* CHRIST, *the* MORE THERE ARE *to* THANK HIM *for* HIS GREAT KINDNESS, *and* *the* MORE *the* LORD *is* GLORIFIED."

2 CORINTHIANS 4:15 (TLB); SEE ALSO JOHN 11:4

YOUR SUCCESS HONORS GOD.

"HONOR *the* LORD *with your* WEALTH ... "

PROVERBS 3:9 (NIV)

"RICHES *and* HONOR COME *from* YOU."

1 CHRONICLES 29:12 (NCV)

"GOD ... *is* GIVING YOU POWER

to MAKE WEALTH ... "

DEUTERONOMY 8:18 (NASB)

Your message, your salvation, your body, your struggles, your success—all proclaim God's glory.

"WHATEVER YOU DO *in* WORD *or* DEED,

DO ALL *in the* NAME *of the* LORD JESUS,

GIVING THANKS THROUGH HIM

to GOD *the* FATHER."

COLOSSIANS 3:17 (NASB)

He's the source; we are the glass. He's the light; we are the mirrors. He sends the message; we mirror it. We rest in his pack awaiting his call. And when placed in his hands, we do his work. It's not about us; it's all about him.

Mr. Tweed's use of a mirror led to a rescue.

May God's use of us lead to millions more.